ETHICS IN OCCUPATIONAL HEALTH AND SAFETY

EMPOWERING ETHICAL CHOICES FOR A SAFER AND RESPONSIBLE FUTURE

AHMED AJMAL | GRAD IOSH | MIIRSM

Made with ♥ on the Notion Press Platform
www.notionpress.com

"I would like to dedicate this book to my father, **Mr. Tajdar Hussain Ansari**, *whose unwavering support and encouragement have been the driving force behind my professional achievements. His guidance, wisdom, and love have been a constant source of inspiration to me, and I owe him a debt of gratitude that can never be repaid."*

"I would also like to dedicate this book to my daughter, **Fazeela Ajmal**, *whose infectious enthusiasm and boundless curiosity continue to inspire me every day. She is a reminder that the work we do in promoting occupational health and safety is not just for ourselves, but for future generations."*

"Finally, I dedicate this book to all the health and safety professionals around the globe who work tirelessly to ensure the safety and wellbeing of their colleagues. Your dedication, expertise, and passion are making a positive impact in workplaces around the world, and your work is more important than ever."

Contents

Foreword *vii*

Preface *ix*

Acknowledgements *xi*

Prologue *xiii*

1. Introduction To Ethics In Health And Safety 1
2. Professional Responsibility And Integrity 5
3. Risk Assessment And Management 7
4. Workplace Culture And Behavior 9
5. Confidentiality And Privacy 12
6. Professional Relationships And Communication 14
7. Social Responsibility And Sustainability 16
8. Case Studies And Ethical Dilemmas 18
9. Conclusion And Future Directions 20

References 23

Feedback 25

Laws And Standard References 27

Foreword

"As the world of work continues to evolve, so too must our approach to occupational health and safety. In today's globalized business environment, companies are under increasing pressure to provide a safe and healthy workplace, not just as a legal obligation, but as a moral imperative.

This book on ethics in occupational health and safety, written by Ahmed Ajmal, an esteemed member of the IOSH Committee, provides a much-needed guide to the ethical principles that should underpin all efforts to ensure workplace safety. By emphasizing the importance of ethics in this field, Ajmal highlights the critical role that businesses and organizations have in protecting the wellbeing of their employees.

This book draws on expert interviews, case studies, and the latest research to provide practical guidance on identifying and mitigating risks, promoting employee wellbeing, and ensuring compliance with relevant regulations and standards. It is a valuable resource for anyone interested in the ethical dimensions of occupational health and safety, and I highly recommend it to all professionals in this field."

Dr. Ahmed Faisal Ansari

Lead Auditor Health & Safety
Saudi Aramco

" "

Preface

"

The health and safety profession plays a vital role in protecting individuals and communities from harm. Health and safety professionals are responsible for identifying and managing risks, promoting safe work practices, and ensuring compliance with legal and ethical standards.

The purpose of this book is to provide a comprehensive overview of the ethics of health and safety practice. The book examines the key ethical issues facing health and safety professionals, including professional responsibility, risk assessment and management, workplace culture and behavior, confidentiality and privacy, professional relationships and communication, social responsibility and sustainability, and ethical dilemmas.

Each chapter is structured to provide a clear and concise analysis of the ethical considerations in each area of health and safety practice. The book includes case studies and real-world examples to illustrate the ethical challenges facing health and safety professionals and to provide strategies for addressing these challenges.

This book is intended for health and safety professionals, students, and educators who are interested in developing a deeper understanding of the ethical considerations in health and safety practice. We hope that this book will contribute to ongoing ethical reflection and professional development in the health and safety profession, and ultimately, to the promotion of safe and ethical practices in the workplace and in the wider community."

Acknowledgements

"I would also like to extend my appreciation to the Institution of Occupational Safety and Health (IOSH), for their ongoing efforts to promote workplace health and safety around the world.

Their commitment to advancing the field through research, education, and advocacy has been a constant source of inspiration to me, and I am honored to be associated with this esteemed organization.

Once again, I would like to express my sincere gratitude to all those who supported me in the creation of this book, and to everyone who is committed to making our workplaces safer, healthier, and more ethical."

Acknowledgements

Prologue

"In today's globalized and highly competitive business environment, occupational health and safety are crucial ethical considerations that must be taken seriously. Employers must provide a safe and healthy workplace, not only as a legal obligation but also as a moral imperative. However, employees also have a responsibility to promote a culture of safety and prioritize their own wellbeing. This book provides comprehensive guidance on the ethical principles that underpin workplace health and safety, drawing on expert interviews, case studies, and the latest research. It offers practical strategies for identifying and mitigating risks, promoting employee wellbeing, and ensuring compliance with relevant regulations and standards."

CHAPTER ONE

Introduction to Ethics in Health and Safety

Ethics in health and safety is important because the decisions and actions of individuals and organizations can have significant impacts on the health and safety of individuals in the workplace and beyond. Ethical considerations are particularly important in contexts where there are competing interests or where there may be potential conflicts between different ethical values. In such cases, ethical principles and frameworks can help individuals and organizations make decisions that balance competing interests and prioritize the well-being of individuals.

Some key ethical principles that are relevant to health and safety include:

- Respect for autonomy: individuals should have the right to make decisions about their own health and safety and should be given the information and resources they need to make informed decisions.
- Beneficence: individuals and organizations have a duty to promote the well-being and safety of others, and to take actions that minimize harm and maximize benefits.

- Non-maleficence: individuals and organizations have a duty to avoid causing harm to others.

Justice: individuals and organizations have a duty to treat others fairly and equitably, and to distribute resources and benefits in a just manner.

Importance of ethics in the health and safety profession

Ethics play a crucial role in the health and safety profession for several reasons:

Protecting individuals: Ethics in health and safety helps to protect individuals from harm and ensure that their health and safety needs are prioritized. By following ethical principles and guidelines, health and safety professionals can make decisions that prioritize the well-being of individuals and prevent unnecessary harm.

- *Maintaining trust*: Health and safety professionals are often responsible for the safety and well-being of others. By acting ethically and responsibly, they can maintain the trust of the individuals they serve and build strong relationships with them.
- *Legal compliance*: Many ethical principles and guidelines in the health and safety profession are also reflected in legal requirements and regulations. By following ethical principles, health and safety professionals can ensure that they follow legal requirements and avoid legal repercussions.
- *Reputation*: Health and safety professionals and organizations that prioritize ethics and responsible behavior often have a positive reputation in their community and industry. This can lead to increased trust, respect, and business opportunities.
- *Moral responsibility*: Health and safety professionals have a moral responsibility to protect the well-being of individuals and prevent harm. By following ethical principles, they can fulfill this responsibility and contribute to a safer and healthier society.

Ethical frameworks and theories

There are several ethical frameworks and theories that can be applied in the context of health and safety. Some of the most common ones are:

- *Utilitarianism*: This ethical theory focuses on maximizing the overall well-being or happiness of individuals. In the context of health and safety, this would mean making decisions that promote the greatest good for the greatest number of people.
- *Deontology*: This ethical theory emphasizes the duty or obligation to do what is right, regardless of the consequences. In the context of health and safety, this would mean making decisions that prioritize the safety and well-being of individuals, even if it is not the most convenient or profitable choice.
- *Virtue ethics*: This ethical theory focuses on developing and embodying positive character traits, such as honesty, compassion, and fairness. In the context of health and safety, this would mean making decisions that reflect these positive character traits and promote the well-being of individuals.
- *Justice*: This ethical framework focuses on fairness and equity and ensuring that individuals are treated equally and given what they are owed. In the context of health and safety, this would mean making decisions that distribute resources and benefits fairly and prioritize the needs of disadvantaged or vulnerable individuals.
- *Care ethics*: This ethical theory emphasizes the importance of caring for others and forming meaningful relationships. In the context of health and safety, this would mean making decisions that prioritize the safety and well-being of individuals and show empathy and compassion for those affected by decisions.

These ethical frameworks and theories can be useful tools for health and safety professionals in making decisions and resolving ethical dilemmas. By understanding and applying these frameworks, they can ensure that their decisions prioritize the well-being and safety of individuals while also considering other relevant ethical considerations.

CHAPTER TWO

Professional Responsibility and Integrity

Professional responsibility and integrity are critical components of occupational health and safety. As an occupational health and safety professional, you have a duty to uphold high ethical standards, act with integrity, and maintain a strong commitment to your profession.

Professional ethics and codes of conduct in health and safety are crucial for ensuring that individuals working in this field uphold the highest standards of ethical behavior and conduct. Health and safety professionals play a critical role in protecting the health and well-being of individuals, communities, and the environment, and it is therefore essential that they act in an ethical and responsible manner.

The professional codes of conduct in health and safety typically cover a range of issues, including:

- *Responsibility*: Health and safety professionals are responsible for ensuring that workplaces are safe and healthy for workers, and that environmental health hazards are managed appropriately.

- *Competence*: Health and safety professionals are expected to maintain a high level of competence in their area of expertise and to continually update their knowledge and skills.
- *Integrity*: Health and safety professionals must act with honesty and integrity in their dealings with clients, colleagues, and the public.
- *Confidentiality*: Health and safety professionals must respect the confidentiality of sensitive information related to their clients or employers.
- *Conflict of interest*: Health and safety professionals must avoid any conflicts of interest that may compromise their ability to act in the best interests of their clients or employers.
- *Professionalism*: Health and safety professionals are expected to always behave in a professional manner, and to promote ethical behavior within their profession.

Adherence to these ethical principles and codes of conduct is essential for promoting public trust and confidence in the health and safety profession. Failure to comply with these standards can result in disciplinary action, loss of professional credibility, and legal consequences.

CHAPTER THREE

Risk Assessment and Management

When conducting risk assessment and management, it's important to consider ethical principles such as fairness, transparency, and accountability. Decisions should be based on objective analysis and balanced with the potential impacts on all stakeholders, including employees, the community, and the environment. Communication with stakeholders about the risks and how they are being managed should also be honest and transparent.

Ethical considerations in risk assessment and management

In the context of risk assessment and management, ethical considerations include the obligation to identify and mitigate risks to protect the health and safety of workers and the public, the duty to communicate risk information transparently and accurately, and the responsibility to use the best available science and data to inform risk management decisions. Other ethical considerations may include ensuring that the rights and privacy of individuals are respected, avoiding conflicts of interest, and promoting social justice and equity by considering the potential impact of risk management decisions on vulnerable populations. Additionally, it is important to consider the long-term consequences of risk management decisions and to weigh the potential benefits and harms of different approaches to risk reduction.

Balancing risk and benefit in decision-making

Balancing risk and benefit in decision-making in ethics involves making ethical decisions that take into consideration both the potential risks and benefits associated with a particular action or decision. This involves weighing the potential harm or negative consequences that may arise from a particular course of action against the potential benefits that may be gained.

Ethically, it is important to ensure that the potential benefits of an action or decision outweigh the potential risks. Additionally, it is important to ensure that the risks are minimized as much as possible through effective risk assessment and management strategies. Ultimately, ethical decision-making in risk assessment and management requires careful consideration of all available information and a commitment to doing what is in the best interests of all stakeholders involved.

CHAPTER FOUR

Workplace Culture and Behavior

Workplace culture and behavior play a crucial role in creating and maintaining ethical practices in occupational safety and health (OSH). Ethical behavior in the workplace involves treating others with respect, honesty, fairness, and responsibility. A culture of safety and ethical behavior promotes a healthy work environment that encourages employees to speak up and report safety concerns without fear of retaliation.

Ethical implications of workplace culture and behavior

Workplace culture and behavior can have significant ethical implications in terms of creating a safe and healthy work environment. For instance, if an organization prioritizes productivity over safety, it can lead to ethical concerns as employees are put at risk of harm. Similarly, if there is a culture of bullying or discrimination, it can create an unsafe work environment that can negatively impact employees‘ physical and mental health.

Ethics also come into play when addressing workplace behavior related to misconduct, such as substance abuse, theft, or harassment. Organizations must ensure that appropriate measures are taken to address such behavior while respecting employees' rights and privacy. Additionally, ethical considerations arise when balancing the need to protect employees' health and safety with their right to privacy, such as in the case of medical or health-related information.

An ethical workplace culture should prioritize the safety and well-being of employees while promoting fairness, respect, and inclusivity. This includes ensuring that employees are trained in ethical behavior and that any concerns related to workplace behavior or culture are appropriately addressed. Ultimately, promoting ethical workplace culture and behavior can lead to a healthier, more productive, and more fulfilling work environment for all employees.

Promoting ethical behavior in the workplace

Promoting ethical behavior in the workplace is essential to create a healthy and safe work environment. Organizations must prioritize the safety and well-being of employees while also fostering a culture of respect, inclusivity, and fairness. Here are some strategies that organizations can use to promote ethical behavior in the workplace:

- *Establish a Code of Conduct*: A code of conduct sets out the organization's expectations for ethical behavior and provides guidance on how to handle ethical dilemmas. Employees should be trained on the code of conduct and reminded of it regularly.
- *Encourage Open Communication*: Employees should feel comfortable reporting any ethical concerns or violations without fear of retaliation. The organization should establish channels for reporting and investigate any concerns promptly.
- *Provide Ethics Training*: Employees should be trained in ethical behavior, including how to recognize and handle ethical dilemmas. This training should be ongoing to ensure that employees are aware of the organization's expectations.
- *Lead by Example*: Leaders in the organization must model ethical behavior and ensure that they are held accountable for their

actions. Leaders must also enforce ethical behavior among their team members.

- *Recognize and Reward Ethical Behavior*: Organizations should acknowledge and reward employees who demonstrate ethical behavior. This reinforces the organization's commitment to ethical behavior and encourages others to follow suit.

CHAPTER FIVE

Confidentiality and Privacy

Confidentiality and privacy are important ethical considerations in OSH. Organizations must respect employees‘ rights to privacy while balancing the need to protect their health and safety. Adequate measures must be taken to ensure confidentiality of health-related information.

Maintaining confidentiality and privacy in health and safety practice

Maintaining confidentiality and privacy in health and safety practice is important to uphold ethical principles. Employees have a right to privacy, including their medical or health-related information, which must be protected. Organizations must ensure that appropriate measures are taken to safeguard such information while balancing the need to protect employees' health and safety. Ethical considerations also arise when dealing with workplace behavior related to misconduct, such as substance abuse or harassment, where employees‘ rights to privacy must be respected while addressing such behavior appropriately. In summary, maintaining confidentiality and privacy is essential in promoting ethical behavior and creating a safe and healthy work environment.

Ethical considerations in sharing health and safety information

Sharing health and safety information can pose ethical dilemmas in terms of confidentiality and privacy. OSH professionals must ensure that they adhere to ethical standards and legal requirements when collecting, storing, and sharing health and safety information. This includes obtaining consent from employees before collecting and sharing their information, limiting access to confidential information only to those with a legitimate need to know, and maintaining the security and confidentiality of the information. Additionally, organizations must have policies and procedures in place to ensure that employees' rights to privacy and confidentiality are respected while still ensuring a safe and healthy workplace. OSH professionals should also provide appropriate training and education to employees on the importance of confidentiality and privacy in health and safety practices.

CHAPTER SIX

Professional Relationships and Communication

Professional relationships and communication are crucial in promoting ethical practice in OSH. Clear and honest communication and respect for privacy and confidentiality foster trust and promote a healthy and safe work environment for all.

Ethical considerations in professional relationships and communication

In the field of occupational safety and health (OSH), ethical considerations are crucial in maintaining professional relationships and communication. OSHA guidelines require honesty, accuracy, and respect in all communications. Construction industry professionals must maintain transparency and ensure that all parties involved are informed of potential hazards. Ethical communication involves respecting the privacy of employees and ensuring that all information is accurate and truthful. Ultimately, ethical communication promotes trust, accountability, and a safer work environment.

Balancing the interests of stakeholders

Balancing the interests of stakeholders involves considering the needs and priorities of various groups who have a stake in or interest in an organization's activities, decisions, and outcomes. Here are 5 ethical points to explain the concept:

- *Recognize and prioritize stakeholders*: Ethics requires that we recognize the interests and concerns of all stakeholders, including employees, customers, suppliers, shareholders, and the wider community. All stakeholders' interests must be prioritized, and decisions made with their interests in mind.
- *Transparency and communication*: Communication is vital to balancing the interests of stakeholders. Organizations must be transparent in their decision-making and communicate openly and honestly with stakeholders about how decisions will affect them.
- *Fairness and equity*: Decisions should be made with fairness and equity in mind, ensuring that all stakeholders are treated equally and with respect. Organizations must avoid favoring one group of stakeholders over another and ensure that everyone's interests are considered.
- *Compliance with laws and regulations*: Organizations must comply with all relevant laws and regulations, including those related to health and safety, labor rights, and environmental protection. They must also ensure that their actions align with ethical standards and do not cause harm to any stakeholder.
- *Continuous improvement*: Organizations must continuously monitor and evaluate their actions to ensure that they are aligned with ethical standards and stakeholder interests. They should be willing to adjust their policies and practices to better balance stakeholder interests and promote ethical behavior.

CHAPTER SEVEN

Social Responsibility and Sustainability

Social responsibility and sustainability in OSH mean considering the impact of decisions on employees, society, and the environment. Ethical considerations play a crucial role in promoting sustainable practices and ensuring that companies act responsibly towards their stakeholders, minimize harm, and contribute positively to society and the environment.

Health and safety professionals and social responsibility

Health and safety professionals have a significant role to play in promoting social responsibility and sustainability within an organization. They are responsible for identifying and managing risks associated with the organization's operations that may impact employees, the environment, or the broader community.

Ethical considerations arise in balancing the interests of different stakeholders and ensuring that the organization operates in a socially responsible and sustainable manner. This includes taking steps to minimize the organization's environmental footprint, promoting diversity and inclusion, and ensuring that workers' rights are respected.

Health and safety professionals can also promote social responsibility and sustainability by engaging with stakeholders, including employees, customers, suppliers, and the local community. This can involve collaborating with stakeholders to identify and address health and safety risks, promoting open communication, and fostering a culture of transparency and accountability.

Promoting sustainability in health and safety practice

Promoting sustainability in health and safety practice is important for ethical reasons. It involves minimizing waste, conserving resources, and protecting the environment. This can be achieved through the following:

- Consider the long-term impact of decisions and actions on the environment and the health and safety of workers and the community.
- Implement sustainable practices such as reducing waste, conserving resources, and using eco-friendly products to minimize the negative impact on the environment.
- Educate and involve employees in sustainability efforts to promote a culture of responsibility and accountability.
- Ensure transparency in reporting environmental and health and safety information to stakeholders.
- Promote sustainability through ethical communication and engagement with stakeholders and the community.

CHAPTER EIGHT

Case Studies and Ethical Dilemmas

Case studies and ethical dilemmas provide valuable insights into ethical decision-making and help health and safety professionals understand the complex nature of ethical issues. They enable professionals to develop critical thinking skills and make informed decisions in challenging situations.

Examining real-world ethical dilemmas in health and safety practice

One example of an ethical dilemma in health and safety practice is the case of a construction company that is under pressure to meet a tight deadline for a project. The company's safety officer identifies several safety hazards at the worksite that could potentially lead to serious injuries or fatalities. However, the project manager insists that the work must continue to meet the deadline.

In this situation, the safety professional faces an ethical dilemma. They must balance the need to ensure the safety and well-being of the workers with the pressure to complete the project on time. Some possible courses of action include:

- Refusing to allow work to continue until the safety hazards are addressed, even if it means missing the deadline.
- Trying to negotiate a compromise with the project manager that addresses the safety hazards while still meeting the deadline.

- Reporting the situation to higher-ups in the company or regulatory agencies, which could result in delays, fines, or other consequences.

Each of these options has ethical implications and potential consequences, highlighting the importance of careful consideration of all stakeholders and ethical principles in making decisions related to health and safety in the workplace.

Strategies for addressing ethical challenges

Strategies for addressing ethical challenges in health and safety practice may include:

- Developing a code of ethics: This can provide guidance on expected ethical behavior and help employees navigate ethical dilemmas.
- Providing training and education: This can help employees recognize and respond to ethical challenges and provide a framework for ethical decision-making.
- Encouraging open communication: This can create an environment where employees feel comfortable raising ethical concerns without fear of retaliation.
- Establishing a reporting system: This can allow employees to report ethical concerns or violations without fear of retribution.
- Implementing consequences for ethical violations: This can promote accountability and deter unethical behavior.

It is important to note that these strategies may not address every ethical challenge and that each situation may require a unique approach. Regular review and evaluation of ethical practices can also help identify areas for improvement.

CHAPTER NINE

Conclusion and Future Directions

In conclusion, ethical considerations play a crucial role in ensuring the effectiveness and success of occupational health and safety practices. Professionals in this field must prioritize the safety and well-being of employees while balancing the interests of stakeholders and promoting sustainability. They must also maintain confidentiality and privacy, foster ethical workplace culture and behavior, and address ethical challenges in a proactive and effective manner.

Moving forward, it is important to continue to integrate ethical considerations into occupational health and safety practices. This can be achieved by providing ongoing education and training for professionals in the field, promoting ethical leadership and decision-making, and regularly reviewing and updating codes of conduct and ethical guidelines. By doing so, we can ensure that occupational health and safety practices remain effective, responsible, and sustainable for the benefit of all stakeholders.

The importance of ongoing ethical reflection and professional development

The importance of ongoing ethical reflection and professional development in health and safety practice cannot be overstated. As the field of OSH evolves, so do the ethical challenges and dilemmas that professionals face. Ongoing ethical reflection allows for the examination and resolution of ethical issues as they arise, helping to prevent harm to individuals and organizations.

Additionally, ongoing professional development helps OSH professionals stay up to date with advancements in the field, including changes to regulations, best practices, and new technologies. This knowledge can be critical in addressing ethical challenges in a timely and effective manner. It also helps professionals to make informed decisions that prioritize the safety and well-being of employees and the community.

In summary, ongoing ethical reflection and professional development are essential components of responsible and effective health and safety practice. It is crucial that professionals continue to engage in self-reflection, education, and dialogue to ensure that they are equipped to handle the complex ethical challenges of the field.

Future directions for ethics in health and safety practice.

As health and safety practices continue to evolve, so do the ethical considerations that come with them. Some future directions for ethics in health and safety practice include:

- *Incorporating emerging technologies*: As new technologies are introduced into the workplace, it's important to consider their ethical implications and ensure that they are used in ways that prioritize safety and protect workers' rights.
- *Addressing global health and safety challenges*: Health and safety professionals will need to consider ethical considerations in the face of global health crises, such as pandemics, and work to ensure that workplaces are safe and healthy for all employees.
- *Fostering a culture of ethical behavior*: Encouraging ethical behavior in the workplace will require ongoing training and communication, as well as the implementation of policies and procedures that prioritize safety and ethical behavior.
- *Promoting sustainability*: As organizations become more aware of the environmental impact of their operations, there will be a growing need to promote sustainable practices in health and

safety, such as reducing waste and using eco-friendly materials.

Collaboration and stakeholder engagement: Health and safety professionals will need to engage with a variety of stakeholders, including employees, management, and regulatory bodies, to ensure that ethical considerations are considered at all levels of decision-making. Collaboration can also help to identify and address ethical challenges before they become major issues.

Overall, the future of ethics in health and safety practice will require ongoing reflection, adaptation, and collaboration to ensure that workplaces remain safe and healthy for all employees.

References

- Gostin, L. O., & Powers, M. (2018). What does social justice require for the public's health? Oxford University Press.
- Kass, N. E. (2001). An ethics framework for public health. American Journal of Public Health, 91(11), 1776-1782.
- Last, J. M. (Ed.). (2007). Public health and human ecology. Appleton & Lange.
- Resnik, D. B. (2015). The ethics of research with human subjects: Protecting people, advancing science, promoting trust. Springer.
- Thompson, D. F. (2016). The ethics of clinical research: Past and present. Cambridge University Press.
- Winkler, E. C., & Coeling, H. V. (2014). Occupational safety and health law. Carolina Academic Press.
- Fleming, M., & Lardner, R. (Eds.). (2019). Ethics and Law for Health Professions. McGraw-Hill Education.

Feedback

"Your Feedback Matters: Let Me Know What You Think about Ethics in Health and Safety"

"*Congratulations on finishing the book on ethics in health and safety! As a writer, I understand the importance of feedback, and I would love to hear your thoughts on my work. Did you find the book informative? Did it make you think differently about ethical considerations in the healthcare and safety professions? Were there any parts that you found particularly helpful or thought-provoking?*

Your feedback is valuable to me, and it will help me improve my writing for future projects. Please feel free to send your feedback to **erahmed69@gmail.com**. *I appreciate your time and your support, and I hope that this book has been a valuable resource for you in navigating the complex ethical challenges of the health and safety field.*

Thank you for reading, and I look forward to hearing from you."

Best regard's

Ahmed Ajmal, Grad IOSH, MIIRSM
IOSH Committee Member

Laws And Standard References

- OSHA (Occupational Safety and Health Administration). (2020). Code of Ethics for Occupational Safety and Health Professionals.
- International Labour Organization. (2016). Occupational safety and health and the prevention of occupational accidents and diseases.
- UNESCO (United Nations Educational, Scientific and Cultural Organization). (2015). Ethical Principles inHealthCare.
- UNICEF (United Nations Children's Fund). (2016). The UNICEF Code of Conduct.
- WHO (World Health Organization). (2017). Global strategy on occupational health for all: The way to health at work.

9 798890 260987

Printed by Libri Plureos GmbH in Hamburg,
Germany